The Journey of Grief

A Simple Book on
What to Expect and How to Move Forward

Ray A. Johnson

Printed in the United States of America

The Ezekiel Group Ministry

DEDICATION

This book is dedicated to my beautiful wife, Lauri. She has faithfully walked with me through many losses, always strong in her love for God and for me. She is the love of my life. I thank God for her and the 39 plus years of marriage that we have shared together. She is a gift from God!

TABLE OF CONTENTS

INTRODUCTION

People often ask me, "What makes you an expert on grief?" The truth is, I'm not. I'm just a pastor with 40 years of experience walking with others in grief, and walking through it in my own life. In 40 years of pastoring, and serving as a fire and hospice chaplain, I've seen a lot of deaths and comforted a lot of people (160 deaths per year as a hospice chaplain alone).

And like you, I've faced loss and death myself. Early in our marriage God blessed my wife and I with two children. But the next two pregnancies ended in heartache as we lost both babies back-to-back. It was a pain like my wife and I had never experienced before. I found myself at a loss on how to "fix" or heal my wife's hurt. In these later years, Lauri and I have experienced the loss of both of our fathers, my mom, and her grandmother. Three of those four deaths occurred within six months of each other.

But my losses haven't always been death. As a pastor I have faced the hurt and heartache of being forced out of a church, twice. They were twenty years apart, but both involved leaders struggling to gain control with lies and deceit. During these times, I found that I struggled with many of the same emotions as I did when I faced the death of a loved one.

In the midst of my dad's illness and ultimate death, I wrote a 6-week grief support class curriculum to minister to my community. Since that time, hundreds and hundreds of people have gone through the class and have found healing and hope. People began asking for that class in writing. Thus, **The Journey of Grief** was born. It is a simple, easy to read book that provides an honest look at the journey, with all of its emotions and effects. But the book also provides hope and healing, sharing what keeps the pain alive and how to move forward.

I'm sorry that you're facing loss, but I'm glad that you picked up this book. I'm praying for you... that God will heal your hurt, make His peace and presence known, and lead you by His Spirit and His Word.

This book is written primarily focused on grief that comes from the death of a loved one, but know that the principles and truths apply much broader than that. If you've experienced the loss of a relationship (through divorce or abandonment), the loss of your job, or the loss of your health, you will see yourself in these pages. Know that there is hope and healing for you, too.

For people who might want to use this book to lead a 6-week grief support class themselves, I've added a "Leader's Guide" at the end.

TRUTHS OF GRIEF

Even though deaths and circumstances are different, in my years of ministry I've learned that there are certain truths that show up in loss again and again. These truths are foundational and will help you navigate your journey of grief and find hope and healing along the way. I hope you will keep them in mind as you walk this journey. Let me share with you what I've seen...

You MUST go through grief

The first truth I've learned is that you must go through grief. A lot of people try to avoid it--to go around it, over it, or under it. But it never works.

I get it; I really do. It hurts...maybe more than any other pain you've ever known. But those who try to avoid it end up letting it pile up like water behind a dam ...and eventually that dam breaks. When the dam breaks, the grief comes barreling out at an overwhelming rate, and at the most unexpected times. Sometimes, grief is so overwhelming that it brings harm to them and the ones they love. Let me share a strong example with you from my own ministry:

On that day of her loved one's death, she wept and wailed in her grief. I can still hear her crying out at the top of her lungs outside of her home—it rang through the countryside.

Initially, she came to a grief class, but after one session she decided she didn't need it. She worked hard to convince herself and others that she would be just fine. She began to push others away, insisting that she was "doing great." But she wasn't. She began to isolate herself and secretly spiral into depression.

I got a call late one night. She was crying uncontrollably. No matter how hard I tried, I couldn't understand what she was saying... Finally, I was able to get her calm enough that I could hear her words. "I don't want to live anymore without him. I'd rather die!" She went on to tell me that she had been drinking all afternoon and had taken "all of the pills she could find." I called 911 and headed her way as quickly as I could. I arrived just behind the deputy sheriff and ambulance. There she laid motionless in the front yard... Miraculously, she was still alive.

They rushed her to the hospital, and she made it. In God's mercy, she lived and began to get the help she needed. Later, she would admit that she had made a mistake—acting as if everything was okay when it wasn't. She realized that she had denied her grief and pain, until it was too much.

Today, she is doing well. God has healed her hurt and has brought her hope and healing.

Don't make the mistake she did—letting the grief pile up behind the dam, trying to ignore the pain.

God made us to grieve for those we love. The Bible is full of people grieving. When we lose one we love, there is deep hurt. To deny that is to short-circuit how God made us.

I've learned it is better to deal with the grief bit by bit, from the very beginning—to cry out to God, to lean on trusted friends, to reach out to others. That's one reason I began leading a grief care class several years ago. It has become a safe place for people to walk through grief together--to find understanding and hope.

Grief is a process

Grief is a process; it's a journey. It is not something that you can schedule or flip a switch and it's over. It's not something that you can give "5-Steps" and then you're finished. As you walk through grief, step by step, God brings healing. Because it's a process, you must learn to walk "step by step" in trust. Sometimes it's one day at a time...sometimes it's one minute at a time. This book will help you walk through that process and know that God will always walk with you!

There is no calendar or exact time

A third truth I've learned is that there is no calendar or exact time for grief. One of the questions I'm often asked is, "When will this end?!" The truth is, I can't tell you. I wish I could. I wish I could tell you that this will be over in 6 months or 1 year (it would be much easier; we can endure almost anything for a while). But I can't. There are so many different factors, and people grieve so differently. Because of that, there is no "calendar" or "schedule" for grief. I can tell you that it will get better (I've seen it again and again!). Healing will take place.

Because there's no "calendar" or "set time," it's important to take it ONE STEP AT A TIME! This is one of the most important lessons that you will learn! It is a day-by-day, sometimes an hour-by-hour journey. If you look too far ahead, it will become overwhelming, especially early on. So, you take one step. Then, if you can, you take another step. In the beginning, they will be "baby steps," and that's okay. It might be just getting out of bed for the day or remembering to eat something. One step at a time!

Sometimes, people ask me, "Will it ever end?" In one sense, grief is never completely over. It stays with you the rest of your life, but not at the same level. The pain does get better. God heals the hurt. The tears turn to smiles, and in time, even laughter. The psalmist writes, "...weeping may endure for a night, but joy comes in the morning" (Psalm 30:5). That verse isn't meant to make light of your grief, but to give you hope. I've seen that hope become reality again and again.

Know that you will not have to walk this journey alone--God will walk with you every step of the way (see Psalm 23 and other verses in the back of the book)!

"To love deeply is to grieve deeply"

Sometimes people feel bad about crying or grieving, especially if they are a Christian or a person of faith. But they shouldn't. We see tears and grief all through Scripture and in life. When we love someone and lose them, part of us is "torn away."

I remember when I was a kid, I did something really dumb (well, I probably did a lot of dumb things)—I decided to lick the metal ice tray out of the freezer. That was a bad idea! My tongue became stuck to it immediately. I couldn't find my mom, and I wasn't going to tell my brothers. So, there was only one thing left to do...pull it off. Boy, did that hurt! Part of my tongue was left on the ice tray, and my tongue was bleeding like crazy!

In a way, death is like that. Part of you is torn away—and that hurts! When God talks about marriage, He says that the two become one. No wonder it hurts when you lose a loved one. You can't expect to become emotionally, physically, and spiritually one and not expect it to hurt when your loved one dies. The Bible is full of men and women who grieved deeply when they lost ones they loved. Jesus Himself cried and was "troubled in spirit" when Lazarus died (see John 11).

I think part of the guilt from grieving as a Christian comes from a misunderstanding or misteaching of Paul's words in the Bible where he tells us, "not to grieve like the rest who have no hope" (1 Thess 4:13-14). Paul's not saying that we can't grieve. Rather, he's saying when we grieve, we grieve with hope—remembering where our loved one is—in God's presence, completely new. It's okay to grieve; in fact, God made us to grieve.

Waves of grief and triggers

In the journey of grief, we will face both waves and triggers of grief.

Triggers of grief occur when we see, hear, taste, smell, or experience something that takes us back to memories of our loved one. Here are some that I have heard and experienced:

- Holidays and special events: Christmas, Thanksgiving, birthdays, anniversaries, graduations, etc.
- Songs/music: you might turn on the radio, walk into a store, or walk into church and hear a song that was one of your favorites, has special memories, or was sung at the memorial service.
- Locations: you might drive past your loved one's favorite restaurant and remember all the meals and times of sharing together; home; workplace; hospital; funeral home; nursing home/rehab facility; church; etc.
- Pictures: social media might pop up a "memory" picture, and you are transported back in time, when you were together; pictures on the wall or in your house; pictures on your phone.
- Smells: cologne, perfume, baking, that "Granny" smell at her home, etc.

Triggers of grief are just what they sound like—triggers that bring back memories of when your loved one was still here. With those memories come all kinds of emotions; some are overwhelming (we will talk about those next). Often, you are caught off guard and wrongly become embarrassed by your emotions and the trigger's impact on you. As you read through this book, you will learn how to deal with these triggers.

Unlike triggers of grief, **waves of grief** can come out of nowhere! When they come, they often knock you off your feet like an unexpected wave hitting you in the ocean. You are overwhelmed by tears and sorrow. At times like this, one often needs to find a place to slip away, a place to cry and reach out to God for comfort and peace.

There will be good days and bad days

Grief is often a roller coaster. There will be good days and bad days, good hours and bad hours. This is especially true early on; but it will continue throughout your grief journey.

There will be days that you wake up and everything seems fine, but then it all becomes a struggle because of a grief trigger, or a "wave of grief" that hits you unexpectedly.

There will be days that just start out bad, and you can tell that it's going to be "one of those days." On days like that, "survival" is the goal. I remember coaching my kids' soccer teams, and there were some days that the kids couldn't tell their left from their right and would kick the ball into their own goal! On days like that, I could either fight against it or just accept that it was "one of those days." Grief is often like that. When those kinds of days happen, be honest about it and hold on to God more than ever.

Moving forward doesn't mean forgetting

Sometimes people are afraid to move forward, because they're afraid that they will forget their loved one. They're afraid that if they enjoy an outing, laugh, or go an hour without thinking of their loved one that they are no longer mourning—and that means that they no longer love their loved one like they should. But that's simply not true! One doesn't have to remain in tears or darkness to prove their love. One can still hold on to their love and move forward.

Moving forward doesn't mean forgetting. It is possible to maintain a bond with the one you lost and still make new memories, experience new adventures, and even form new friendships and relationships.

Much life has happened since the loss of our two children early in our marriage, and even since the loss of both my parents. But I still remember and cherish our babies and my parents. I haven't forgotten them at all. In fact, sometimes their loss seems like it was just yesterday.

Grief is different for everyone

Grief is different for everyone because deaths are different, circumstances are different, and we are different. Some deaths are long and drawn out; some are sudden and unexpected. The death may occur in isolation, or it may occur in the midst of a whole storm of circumstances.

Personalities are different too. Some of us are very emotional, and some of us are stoic and "matter of fact." Some of us wear our emotions on our sleeves, and some of us are quiet and reserved.

Because these factors are so different, we shouldn't compare our grief to someone else's. This often leads to false guilt or questions about if we're "doing it right." I've had people ask me, "My friend dreamed about their loved one almost immediately, and it's been a year and I haven't. Is something wrong?" Or "My friend cries every day, but I can't cry anymore. Does that mean that I don't love my spouse or miss them like I should?" No, nothing's wrong; their journey is just different.

Others get frustrated with family and friends because they are not "crying enough" or crying too much...they are too "matter of fact" or seem to have "moved on." The truth is, they're grieving in their own way. Just like you need that freedom to grieve as God made you, they do too.

If one can understand this, it will save a lot of false guilt, heartaches, family fights, and regrets.

THE JOURNEY OF GRIEF

William Worden talks about "Four Tasks of Mourning" (Worden). But I think it's fair to see these as "roads" or patterns in people's journey through grief. They are not straight roads, but rather winding, overlapping roads. These "roads" give a general guideline of where we are and where we need to go. You will see these "roads" woven throughout this book. Here are the four "roads" (tasks).

Accept the reality of the loss

Early on in grief, we are in denial. It might be flat out, blatant denial that the death isn't true; or it might be more subtle. Often in the beginning we walk around like a zombie, going through the motions. We are numb and in disbelief. The death still seems like a bad dream that we wish we could wake up from.

This is very common early on and can even pop up again throughout the journey. We may find ourselves waking up in the middle of the night to check on our loved one, rushing home from shopping because we need to get back, or driving by the hospital or nursing home to visit like we have done for weeks or months. We may "hear" our loved one drive up in the driveway or walking in the house. In the beginning, this is all very normal.

However, this "denial" cannot continue. In time, one must realize that their loved one is gone, that they are not coming back.

I have observed that there seems to be a point in time for everyone when the reality of the death sinks in. We realize that our loved one is not coming back. It comes at different times for different people, but it comes. This is a **key turning point** in our healing. Until this comes, we will make little if any progress in moving forward.

Process the pain

Many people have shared with me the deep, deep pain that comes with the loss of a loved one. They describe it as a pain unlike any other they have ever experienced. Because it is so intense, it becomes a challenge to deal with it, to "make it stop." This was the hardest thing for me when we lost our two babies—how do I fix the hurt in my wife, make the pain stop, and deal with the hurt within me.

Sharing with others is a good place to begin. Your family, a trusted friend, your church, or a grief support class can give you a place to share honestly about the pain and find healing in the midst of it.

Ultimately, however, I found that it is God who has to heal the pain. He knows the hurt and sting of death; He's been there with His own Son. He is the "God of all comfort" and the "Prince of Peace."

Adjust to a world without your loved one

With the loss of your loved one, you are plunged into a whole new world that you didn't ask for and weren't ready for. Your loved one is gone, and with that comes all kinds of changes.

- Physical—who will take care of the house, groceries, care, finances, etc.?
- Emotional—who am I now; where do I find my identity and purpose; where do I find encouragement, comfort, guidance, and hope?
- Spiritual—is God still there; why did He let this happen; my faith is shaken; I feel alone; how do I feel close to God in the midst of the pain?

This is a huge adjustment! It won't happen overnight, and it won't happen alone. God's grace and strength, trusted family or friends, and this book will help you down this road.

Maintain a connection to your lost loved one <u>and</u> move forward in life

This is what we talked about earlier in the book when I said, "moving forward isn't forgetting."

This road brings a lot of questions, like... How do I move forward but still cherish and honor my loved one? How do I find new life but hold on to the memories? How do I keep from becoming anchored to the past and the death of my loved one? How do I hold on to existing relationships and build new relationships without feeling guilty?

This may seem impossible now, but the time will come when you will be ready for this road. God will gently lead you to this point and help you in the midst of it.

Again and again, I have seen God help heal the hurts and bring people to this point. It is here that we begin to see the "mourning turn into joy" (Psalm 30:5).

THE EMOTIONS AND EFFECTS OF GRIEF

Many talk about the "Five Stages of Grief," but I'm not a big fan. First of all, grief doesn't follow a neat pattern or flow easily into "stages." Secondly, there are a whole lot more emotions and effects of grief than five! If you've been there, you know!

Grief is better seen as a tangled ball of emotions and effects. They can come and go, and vary in intensity. There is no way to capture all of them, but here are ones that I see most commonly. I share these so that you will know what to expect, and realize that you're not crazy or losing your mind. Maybe you will recognize a few...

Disbelief, zombie, numb

You may find yourself walking around like a zombie—numb, robotic, and just "going through the motions." You may have taken care of what was needed (including funeral plans) and not even remembered doing it. This is very common, especially in the early months. In fact, I've had people tell me that honestly, they don't really remember much of the funeral; they were just there, numb. Others have shared how they have gone to the store and then wondered how they got there, not remembering driving there at all.

Nightmare or bad dream I wish I would wake up from

Especially in the early stages, the death just doesn't seem real. It seems like a bad dream or a nightmare that you wish you could wake up from. This emotion is very common and part of the early denial of the death. You are still trying to process it all, and you don't want it to be real. You want to wake up the next day and find that everything is back to normal. Unfortunately, it's not.

Blurry thinking, "Jell-O" brain

It's very common for people to struggle with thinking and remembering after a death. Don't worry if you're there. You're not losing your mind or suddenly getting Alzheimer's. I've heard stories of those who have:

- lost their keys (sometimes only to find out they're holding them).
- forgotten to take medicine or eat.
- walked across the room or driven across town, only to forget what they were going there for or where they were going.
- put something up for safekeeping but now can't remember where it is.
- forgotten an appointment or to pay a bill.

You get the idea. During this time, having someone help you, keeping lists, and posting "sticky notes" becomes more important than ever. This is one reason I caution people against making any major decisions in the first year of grief.

I believe that much of this comes because our mind is so preoccupied with grief that we are distracted. Our mind is so overwhelmed by grief that we can't focus on other things.

Anger

Anger is one of the most powerful emotions that people face in grief. Not everyone struggles with it, but many do. For those who do, I've learned that anger is usually directed at one, some, or all of these five people:

- God
- the one who died
- ourselves
- family
- person x—the doctor, the drunk driver, etc.

Often, we become angry at God because "He let our loved one die. He could have stopped it, but He didn't." We prayed and prayed, but our loved one still died. We see God as unloving, uncaring, or weak.

We can become angry at our loved one who died. This might surprise you, but I see it often... and understand. Sometimes I will hear the anger expressed this way, "Why did you leave me all alone! How could you leave me to take care of all this!" We're angry at death and the shattered world it has left us in.

Sometimes, however, we are angry at our loved one because he didn't take care of himself. Maybe our loved one didn't take his meds, eat like he should have, or quit smoking or doing drugs. We might blame our loved one for contributing to their own death and bringing hurt to us.

Surprisingly, sometimes we become angry with ourselves. We blame ourselves for the death. We say things like, "I should have gotten them to the doctor sooner." "I should have gotten a second opinion." "I should have seen the signs sooner." Much of it is false guilt and false thinking that we could have changed the circumstances or stopped it from happening.

Family often becomes the brunt of the anger. Maybe because they are close; maybe because they have added to the hurt; maybe because of past hurts that have already been present in the family for a long time. Grief tends to magnify hurts that are already there.

Finally, we might be angry with "person x"—the doctor who didn't save them or made a mistake; the drunk driver who hit our loved one head on; the hospital who missed the diagnosis or put them off. Often in this anger, there is a demand for justice, and it can turn "ugly" fast.

Bottom line, we are usually angry at death or what we see as "unfair" ... at the circumstance. C.S. Lewis once said,

> *"I sat with anger long enough, until she told me her real name was grief"* (Lewis).

There is much truth in what he shared.

Forgiveness is an important part of this emotion. We will talk about it more in the chapter, "What Keeps the Pain Alive." If you are struggling greatly with this emotion now, you may want to skip ahead to that section and read about forgiveness. There are also several Scriptures at the back of the book about forgiveness.

Relief

This seems odd, but I see it often—especially after a prolonged illness, a struggle with pain and suffering, or the sorrow of watching a loved one struggle with dementia or Alzheimer's. No one likes to see their loved one hurt. So, when death brings an end to the pain and suffering, there is a sense of relief—especially if you know heaven awaits, where everything is made new and perfect.

I also see this relief when long-time caregivers are physically and emotionally exhausted. They are at a point where they are not sure if they can make it one more step or one more hour—much less one more day. So, when their loved ones pass, there is a sense of relief.

But, with both often comes guilt... guilt that they feel relieved or that they somehow hastened the death. But they shouldn't; it's a natural response to seeing the pain of a loved one and the extreme exhaustion of caregiving. They didn't hasten the death or abandon their love for their loved one.

There's nothing wrong with rejoicing that your loved one is in heaven and being relieved that the suffering of this world is finally over. There's nothing wrong with finally finding rest after a long, difficult journey.

In time, I've noticed that even those who experience the emotion of relief have a growing sense of loss. As the feeling of relief gives way to the reality of the death, the pain emerges from the shadows.

What if, if only, guilt

This haunting emotion follows so many...

- If only I had gotten my loved one to the doctor sooner; I should have gotten a second opinion; I should have noticed the change; I should have used a different doctor/hospital.
- I should have stopped her from going; I should have driven myself.
- I should have stayed home; I could have prevented it.
- I'm a nurse/doctor/policeman/EMT, I should have been able to see it/stop it.
- And many, many more thoughts like these...

Most of the guilt we face is "false guilt"—feeling guilty over something we couldn't have known, controlled, or changed.

Occasionally, there is true, rightful guilt. In these rare instances, we must find forgiveness and peace from God. He promises that He is faithful to forgive us and cleanse us from our guilt (1 John 1:9 and Psalm 103).

I have found that often at the root of guilt is the thought or sense that "I can control things, that I somehow have the power to keep something from happening or change the outcome." However, that's simply not true.

None of us have that kind of power. The older I become, and the longer I live, I realize that I control very little. Ironically, that realization has been very freeing, and has helped me find peace and rest.

Extreme pain, loss

Many tell me that they have never felt pain this deep, and for this long. The pain of grief is unlike any other. It goes deep, deep into the soul. The Bible rightfully calls it a "sting." It seems like it will never end, never get better.

The old saying, "Time heals all wounds," has some truth to it, but not completely. Healing does take time, and the harshness and severity of the pain does get better. But there will always be a sense of loss for the one you loved. In time the pain will become bearable, not so overwhelming and so suffocating. The memories that brought tears begin to bring smiles. God is the Great Physician that can heal the hurts. I've seen it in my life, and the lives of others.

I've learned personally, and with others through the years, that ultimately only God can heal the hurt. People can help walk us through the pain...cry with us, comfort us, and pray for us. But, ultimately, only God can heal the pain. That's why it's so important to cry out to Him and spend time with Him.

Loneliness/emptiness

Loneliness and emptiness may be the most common emotion that people facing loss deal with. Loneliness can come when you're alone or when you're in the midst of a hundred people. Often with that loneliness, there is an emptiness, or a void, which seems to overshadow everything.

Loneliness comes because the one you love, that was a part of you, is gone. Part of you is missing. No one or no thing can replace that emptiness.

I ask people in my classes and individual counseling sessions, "When is the loneliest time for you?" By far, the majority of them answer, "Nighttime!" That makes sense. The end of the day is when we finally stand still, and our thoughts catch up with us.

We can stay busy throughout the day, but at some point we have to stop. Then all those emotions and memories come flooding in. Nighttime is also when you and your loved one would catch up with one another, sit down and talk about the day, or just rest in each other's presence. If you were married, nighttime is when you and your spouse would end the day in each other's arms. Now the bed is empty and lonely.

It's not always nighttime though. Some share that it's mealtime, or the morning. I asked one who shared that it was morning, "Why the morning?" She replied, "That's when we sat in the sunroom together, sipping coffee and talking about the day ahead." It was their daily routine. No wonder the morning was so hard!

How do you overcome the loneliness, or the emptiness? There is no simple answer that will change everything overnight. And in one sense, the "missing" and loneliness will always be there. That's part of grief. But there are some truths that help us.

One truth is that as long as we have God, we will never be alone. That's the promise of Psalm 23,

> *"Yea, though I walk through the valley of the shadow of death, I will fear no evil; For <u>You are with me;</u>"*

There is comfort in knowing that ultimately we're never alone. God promises to be with us every step of the way. Again and again, in the Bible the psalmist talks about God's presence and His constant thoughts toward us (like Psalm 40 and 139). I find peace and comfort in that.

I knew a man who was struggling greatly. He just needed to know that God was there. As he was traveling down Interstate-65 he cried out to God in tears, "God I need to know you're here! I need to know that I'm not alone."

As he rolled up behind an 18-wheeler, there written in the dirt on the back of the trailer was, "I AM HERE! -GOD." It doesn't get much clearer than that! God knew he needed to hear from Him. God knew that he needed that assurance. God knows when WE need that, too. If you look around, in little and big ways, God is assuring us that He is here.

There are some practical things that we can do to help with loneliness as well.

- During those lonely times, find something to do: read, craft, exercise, reach out to others, volunteer, etc. Resist the urge to just sit at home and dwell on the loss.
- Allow friends and family to be a part of your life; if you don't have any family or friends nearby, pray that God will bring some into your life (I've seen Him do that).
- Some leave a radio or TV on for voices/sound; I would encourage playing worship music or the old hymns.
- I have found that listening to music at bedtime, or reading and listening to Scripture helps tremendously (Bible apps can read to you).

Punishment

I must admit that punishment wasn't on my first list; I added it after it kept coming up in several of my grief classes. People shared that they felt like God was punishing them for their past, and that He did it by taking their loved one.

I'm sorry if you are one of those who feel that way. Maybe someone taught you that or told you that; maybe you put that on yourself. Just know that doesn't really fit the heart and character of God.

Maybe there is some guilt behind that thinking. It might be something that you've done in the past, or maybe something you should have done, and you didn't. If that's true, know that God can forgive your sins and mistakes.

God is full of mercy and grace. The Bible is full of stories where God forgave people of their sins, and some we would consider really "big sins." For the believer, God promises to forgive you and cleanse you "from all unrighteousness" (1 John 1:9). He promises to remove your sins as far as the east is from the west (Ps 103). Just be honest with Him and ask Him. Please accept and live in that forgiveness. When God has forgiven you, put up a "No Fishing" sign and don't go back.

I might add that often the guilt is a "false guilt." Maybe that is where you are. You may be blaming yourself for something that isn't your fault or that you couldn't have controlled. Do you have a trusted friend, family member, or pastor that you could talk with? Often they can help us know whether the guilt is real or false.

Depression

It makes sense that depression would be a part of loss. Probably everyone, to some degree or another, faces depression in the midst of grief. Some struggle with it at a low level, and some struggle with it in great measure. For some it will be their first experience with depression, and for others it has been a part of their life for a long time.

How do you know if you're struggling with depression? Here are some signs:

- You don't want to get out of bed in the morning; there is no motivation to do anything.
- There's a "dark cloud" or darkness that seeks to pull you in.
- You experience regular feelings of hopelessness, worthlessness, or unending guilt.
- Withdrawing from friends/family becomes the norm.
- You find yourself neglecting self-care.
- You have constant, recurring thoughts of death or suicide.

If you, or someone you love, are struggling with depression, don't be afraid to ask for help. Talk with your friend or family, your pastor, or your doctor. The ongoing stress of death and long-term caregiving can take a physical and mental toll on you that increases your chances of depression. Don't be afraid to ask for help, even if it means meds temporarily. If the need is urgent or you have no one, reach out by phone to the Crisis Suicide Lifeline at 988 (call or text) or call 911.

God can bring light to the darkness; God can bring hope to the hopeless. Don't be afraid to cry out to God in honesty and invite others to cry out with you.

Depression is one reason I warn people again and again about isolation. When we isolate ourselves, it allows the darkness to pour in and overwhelm us. We've all seen the "wild animal" shows where the predator hunts its prey. Its strategy is to isolate one of the animals from the pack and then attack. The Enemy (Satan) works the same way on us. He seeks to isolate us and then drag us into darkness. The Bible tells us that Satan seeks to "steal, kill, and destroy" (John 10:10). Run to God, not away from Him. Keep friends and family close.

Jealousy

You may be thinking, jealousy? What would one be jealous of? What happens when you sit down at a restaurant to eat alone and across the way is a couple enjoying a meal together, snuggled up close and sharing life together? What happens when you drive by a playground or school and see the children laughing and playing? What happens when you watch a graduation and realize your child will never see one?

All of these, and more, can invite jealousy. We may become jealous of what they have, and we no longer have. If we're not careful, this jealousy can turn into bitterness and resentment. It will become a poison to us, and those around us. Shakespeare calls it a "green eyed monster" (Shakespeare). Jealousy and anger often walk hand and hand.

If we focus on what we've lost and no longer have, jealousy will creep in. But, if we focus on the joys, the adventures, and the memories... if we "count our blessings" we will be more likely to live in thankfulness rather than jealousy.

Flashbacks

Flashbacks are more common than you might think. Flashbacks to the scene, the time of death, the moment you heard, the funeral home, and more. Sometimes they occur during the day, and sometimes they wake us up at night.

I had to learn to deal with these as a fire chaplain, having seen some of the most tragic and gruesome deaths you can imagine.

I have found that more than ever it's important that I re-direct my thinking. When a thought or picture comes up in my mind, I have to redirect my thinking to another thought or picture. It helps if I already have that new thought or picture prepared ahead of time. It might be a Scripture, a song, a literal picture on my phone, or a special memory. I have to mentally choose "not to go down that road," and choose another road to go down. I've also found that often I have to physically change location in order to mentally change my direction. I might need to get up and go outside, go for a walk, or get out of bed and sit down to read my Bible.

We will talk about this more in a later chapter. It has proven very effective for those who faithfully try it.

Fear

Fear is a frequent emotion. Fear may come because of the unknown or because your security is gone. I found one lady fearful for her safety with her husband gone, another unsure if she could pay all the bills, and another unsure if she would even have a place to live when her husband passed away. Fear in the midst of loss can be very real.

I encourage those in fear to put their trust in God, the One who promises to care for the widow. The Bible is full of stories of how He provided and protected those under His care.

I have seen this in my own life. When I faced tremendous loss, fear was a constant battle. But I saw God provide again and again. Seeing God provide strengthened my faith and took my fear away. In addition, I spent a lot of time in the Psalms; they constantly reminded me of God's protection and provision.

This doesn't mean that there won't be difficult days, or days where you wonder how you're going to make it. But it does mean that even in those days, God will be there. He will never leave you or abandon you.

Exhaustion

Exhaustion, especially for a long-term caregiver, is very common. Those grieving find themselves physically, emotionally, and spiritually exhausted.

You will, therefore, need rest—physically, emotionally, and spiritually.

To find rest physically and emotionally, some take a brief trip to get away from it all. One lady secured a two-night stay in a neighboring town; others have taken trips to the beach or mountains. Not everyone can do that, or wants to, but you will need to find some way to find rest.

Know, too, that being able to sleep after a loved one passes is often difficult. The weight of grief, the overwhelming needs, and all that dominates our minds when we lay down make it difficult to sleep. Sometimes sleep aids are needed temporarily. Here are some practical things near or at bedtime that help as well:

- Prayer and Bible reading
- Worship music or some of your favorite songs played before or while you sleep

- Keep a notebook nearby to jot down what comes to mind so it can be set aside for tomorrow
- Journal or read a book
- Exercise during the day
- A warm bath or warm drink
- Establish an end of the day, night-time routine

Without rest, it is very difficult to move forward. I pray that you find rest... physical rest, and spiritual rest in Him.

Overwhelmed

Almost everyone tells me that they are overwhelmed by this new, unwanted journey. They are overwhelmed by all the emotions, but also by all the paperwork and new responsibilities that have been thrust on them. Until you've been there, you don't realize all that has to be done after a death... and for many, all alone. It is often like drinking from a fire hydrant... just too much at one time.

It's in times like this that we learn to take it "one step at a time." If we try to tackle too much or run ahead, it will definitely be overwhelming. During my wife's battle with cancer, we began learning to live one day at a time. We had to remind ourselves constantly not to run ahead of God. In fact, that became our mantra: "Don't run ahead of God!"

If you think about it, even the Lord's Prayer ("Our Father") encourages us to live one day at a time:

> "Our Father in heaven,
> Hallowed be Your name.
> Your kingdom come.
> Your will be done
> On earth as it is in heaven.
> *Give us this day our daily bread."* (Matthew 6)

Even in the Old Testament, when God miraculously provided manna from heaven, He told them to gather enough for one day. If they gathered for two days, it spoiled. He was teaching them to trust Him one day at a time. I've learned that God gives the grace and strength for the moment, when it comes.

Because we are overwhelmed, we must also learn to ask for help. Most of us are not good at this (I'm not!). Many of us are "givers." And I've learned that "givers" are not good "receivers." But there are people who genuinely want to help; and the truth is, we need it now more than ever. We may have to help them know how to help us; but we need to let them. Remember what a blessing and joy it is when we help someone? Know that it is for them, too. So, don't rob them of that joy or blessing.

THE CHALLENGES OF DIFFERENT DEATHS

There is a commonness to death, but not every death is the same. Here are some things that I hear in each type of death:

DEATH OF A PARENT

The loss of a parent is one of the most common deaths, and often our first experience with loss up close. There is something special about a mom or a dad.

I've heard people say:

- "I feel like an orphan." I admit that at first I didn't understand this. But now that both of my parents are gone, I do. I still have my family (my wife, kids, grandkids, and brothers), but it's different when the one who gave birth to you and the father who helped raise you are both gone. There's no living connection; there's no gathering place or central "magnet" for the family. The "glue" that holds you together is gone.

- "My security/help/protection is gone." Parents are often the ones who help provide the much-needed encouragement, protection, counsel, and "glue" to the family. When one or both are gone, that sense is eroded or shaken.
- "There were still some things I needed to say or do." It seems like we're never quite ready to let go of our parents. And because we're not quite ready, we often leave things unsaid or undone. Maybe we didn't share our love like we should have or apologize for the hurts and make things right. Now there is guilt, or at the very least a sense that things were left undone.

It becomes even more difficult if it's your last parent. When the first parent passes away, you often still have the comfort and presence of the other. But when both are gone, all that is gone. That generation of your immediate family is gone. You are now the leading generation, and the baton has shifted to you (and your siblings). With that comes new fears and changes in relationships.

Speaking of relationships, the death of a parent(s) often affects your relationships with siblings. Maybe one of your parents was the glue that kept the family together, the peacemaker, or simply the reason to gather. But now all that is gone—and families often begin to drift apart. Sometimes, families even begin to argue and fight with one another, bringing even greater hurt.

DEATH OF A SPOUSE

A lady named Kelley Lynn captured the loss of a spouse well, when she wrote,

> *"The death of a spouse or partner is different than other losses, in the sense that it literally changes every single thing in your world going forward. When your spouse dies, the way you eat changes. The way you watch TV changes. Your friend circle changes (or disappears entirely). Your financial status changes. It effects your self-worth. Your self-esteem. Your confidence. Your rhythms. The*

> *way you breathe. Your mentality. Your brain function. (Ever heard of the term 'widow brain?' If you don't know what that is, count yourself as very lucky). Your physical body. Your hobbies and interests. Your sense of security. Your sense of humor. Your sense of womanhood or manhood. EVERY. SINGLE. THING. CHANGES. You are handed a new life that you never asked for and that you don't particularly want. It is the hardest, most gut-wrenching, horrific, life-altering of things to live with"* (Lynn).

If you're there, you know the hurt and pain. Your entire world has changed.

Sometimes people are taken back by how much it hurts and life changes. But it makes sense. The Bible tells us that in a marriage "the two become one" (Genesis 2:24). You physically, emotionally, and spiritually become one. So, when you lose your spouse, you lose part of yourself. Part of you is torn away. Part of you is missing.

Look at the quote above. Mark those things that stand out most in your life. In that quote are a number of what we call "secondary losses." The primary loss is obviously your wife or husband, but the secondary losses are all the roles they played in your life—cheerleader, best friend, mechanic, counselor/sounding board, etc. Those things you marked are your "secondary losses." "Secondary" doesn't mean they aren't important or don't hurt as much. "Secondary" just means that they are not the person themselves. These secondary losses are a major part of your hurt and grief.

Identity and purpose are major losses in the death of a spouse. People often ask, "Who am I?" or say, "I don't even know why I'm here or what my purpose is." That's normal, and part of the grief journey is figuring that out.

In discovering our identity, we sometimes need to go back to who we were before we were married, looking at what we enjoyed doing but maybe set aside for our spouse. We look at who we were when we were on our own, those rare times when we were away from our loved one. Ultimately, we will find our identity in Christ, and our relationship with Him.

When thinking of your purpose, think about how God made you; how He gifted you. See if there is a pattern through the years like caregiving, encouraging, or serving others. Often this hints at your purpose. God may place you in different roles, but the root purpose can remain the same. I remind people, "Your purpose didn't end with your spouse's death." God still has a purpose for you. I believe that with all my heart.

DEATH OF A SIBLING

For some, this is harder than the loss of a parent. It may seem odd, but I have seen it numerous times.

Often there is a special bond between a brother or a sister that has been built over time, especially among twins. I've had a twin attend my grief classes, and the death of her twin sister was overwhelming. In addition, sometimes the sibling in a larger family played the role of the mother or father. So, the loss of a sibling was like the loss of a parent as well.

In the loss of a sibling, guilt is often a part of the loss:

- Sometimes that guilt comes because the surviving siblings feel like they should have "kept it from happening" or been able to stop it. This is especially true for older siblings who have been the "protector" all their lives. Somehow, they feel like they failed at their job.
- Other times, there is guilt over being the survivor—what some would call "survivor's remorse." They wish it had happened to them rather than their sibling. Some feel like they should have died because they had more health issues or were older.
- Finally, sometimes guilt and regrets come because there was tension or a broken relationship. It may have been years since their last contact or visit. Now they're gone.

Some struggle because the death of a sibling hits too close to home. Maybe they've tried to avoid thinking about death, but now they can't. The death of a sibling reminds them that death is inevitable, and now it's closer than ever. The shortness of life becomes too real. If there have been multiple sibling deaths, they begin to think, "Who's next?" Sometimes this thought can lead to ongoing fear and worry.

The death of a sibling will always change the family "dynamic." Everybody plays a role in the family—maybe a peacemaker, leader/organizer, or the one who is the "glue" to the family. When that person dies, the family relationship shifts. Often the family drifts apart and changes focus. Sometimes, the family begins to fight within.

DEATH OF A CHILD

The death of a child is one of the most difficult deaths to deal with, even for me as a pastor.

We've all probably heard the phrase, or said it ourselves, "A child isn't supposed to die before we do!" In our mind, a person should at least make it to adulthood. It just seems like an "unspoken" rule. With that frustration and sense of "unfairness," often comes anger at God. "How could He be so uncaring? How could He let an innocent child die? I wanted my child, and so many who didn't even want a child have one." We've talked about this anger previously in "The Emotions and Effects of Grief." It is a difficult anger that must be worked through in order to find healing.

Not only do parents blame God, but often they blame themselves. I've heard them, in the midst of tears, cry out "I should have kept this from happening!" "I was supposed to protect them!" They blame themselves for the loss. They are full of guilt.

With the early death, parents begin to grieve "what would have been." They begin to think about the:

- Childhood sports and activities they will never see.

- The graduation they will never be a part of.
- The wedding that will never take place.
- And the grandkids that will never come.

A person once said, *"Grief over the loss of a child is disabling. It will be more intense and last longer than grief over the loss of anyone else. The death of a child has been called the ultimate bereavement"* (Hayes).

It's so hard to find comfort in the loss of a child. The words and thoughts we use to comfort ourselves in the death of an adult, especially an older adult, don't work here. We can't say, "They lived a long, good life." We can't talk about all the years and memories shared together.

In the beginning, the loss of a child is raw and "in your face." It overwhelms you and occupies your every thought. In time, the grief begins to move to the shadows. Not forgotten, but not in every waking thought. It becomes what I call "shadow grief." I have seen this especially with the loss of a child. Parents begin to move forward (because they have to), but the grief lingers in the shadows. It steals their joy, brings a low-level anger or irritability, and often keeps tension in the marriage and family relationship.

I cannot fully imagine the deep, deep loss of a child even though my wife and I have lost two babies... But I do know that God can bring healing. I do know that the light can shine again.

In the Bible, David found comfort in knowing that he would see his child again in heaven (2 Samuel 12:23). David's hope is my hope as well. I often get asked, "Will I see my child in heaven?" I believe that the Bible teaches that you will see your child in heaven. When we understand the mercy and love of God, and see passages like 2 Samuel 12:23, it helps us know that our child will be in God's presence. We will see him there—made completely new (Revelation 21:3-5).

DEATH OF A LOVED ONE BY SUICIDE

Suicide brings such tremendous hurt, guilt, shame, and embarrassment to a family. Sometimes it comes from within, often from without. We can't help but feel betrayed, angry, or abandoned. Few know how to handle it, and it brings almost certain isolation. One lady told me how she would go shopping, and people would see her coming down the aisle, and turn down another aisle rather than face her.

The tragedy leaves a lot of questions...mainly, "Why?!" "How could you do this to me? How could you do this to yourself? Was I to blame? Should I have seen it coming?" And the questions go on and on.

One of the hardest is the "why" question. I can't answer the "why" question completely, but I can give some general answers. In my many years of ministry and dealing with those who are suicidal, I've learned that people usually take their lives for one (or several) of these reasons:

- Tremendous pain. Sometimes it's physical pain, and sometimes it's emotional pain. In chronic illness, sometimes the pain becomes so severe and lasts so long that people feel like they can no longer go on. In their minds, the pain must end, even if it means taking their lives. For some, it isn't chronic illness, but extreme or prolonged emotional pain. The pain is just as real. In fact, "cutters" will tell you that they can handle the physical pain better than the emotional pain; that's why they cut themselves.
- Overwhelming guilt and shame. They believe that they have done something so horribly wrong that neither God nor their loved ones can ever forgive them. They see no way out and can't stand the idea of facing the ones they have hurt, or the world around them.
- Deep darkness. Whether emotional or spiritual, the darkness is overwhelming. Light and hope have been swallowed up. They are being pulled deeper and deeper into darkness like a whirlpool or sinking sand. I have seen teens physically darken their rooms to parallel their deep emotional and spiritual darkness. They would

leave the lights off, close their blinds, and even drape blankets over their windows. They simply mirrored what was in their heart and minds.

- Distorted thinking. I don't mean it harshly, but no one who takes their life is thinking in their "right mind" at that moment. None are thinking like they normally would. Their thoughts have become distorted, confused, and filled with lies of the Enemy (Satan).

History and personal experience show that suicide has a "ripple" effect on others. Like a rock dropped into a pond or skipped across the lake, a tragic death like this brings doubts, shame, and even depression in the survivor(s). Statistics show that once suicide has entered a family, the chances of another suicide greatly increase (Bakian AV). That doesn't mean it has to happen; it just means that the emotional pain and stress it brings to the surviving family can shift one in that direction.

Some "myths" of suicide also make it difficult for the family and increase the sense of guilt. Here are a few of those myths:

- They always leave a note (not true).
- They always give us hints (not true).
- They can always be stopped (not true).

Unfortunately, in my years of ministry I have dealt with many who have threatened to take their lives. Sometimes God has used me (and others) to help them see the light and their lives were spared. But there have been other times when that didn't happen, and they succeeded. There were times when my words of hope and counsel went unheard.

I remember one young man especially... He had reached out to me several times through the years and today seemed no different. We met and began to talk. After spending hours with him, there was a peace and light that shined through the darkness. Finally, I got home after a long day and sat down to watch the local news that night. Guess what the lead story was? A young man who had purposely stepped out in front of a train.

It was the young man I had spent the afternoon with. I was shaken. In the hours, days, and weeks ahead I had to wrestle through some of those same questions you have had to wrestle through: What if...? I should have... if only I had... In the end, I had to realize that I had done all that I could. I had loved on him, shared hope with him, and prayed fervently for him. I had to realize in the end that I could not stop him.

Suicide becomes more difficult because nobody wants to talk about it. Few want to talk about grief, period; but imagine if your grief involves suicide. In this sense, your grief will be even more difficult. You will have to work hard not to become isolated. Don't let darkness swallow you up as well.

WHAT KEEPS THE PAIN ALIVE

Through the years, I noticed that the pain for some seemed to linger longer. I wondered why and began to pray and watch. Here are some factors that I began to notice:

False Thinking

We all face a "battle of the mind" at some time or another. But during times of grief and loss, this seems to grow tremendously. During this time, we must learn to re-direct our thinking, to turn away from false thinking to right thinking.

Picture it this way... If we go out the door and walk to the barn on the same path every day, what will happen? That's right, we will wear a path on the grass and eventually make it a rut. That's what our minds do. It wears a rut into our thinking, and our minds "automatically" go there. But what if we took a different path to the barn, and started doing that every day? Eventually the old path would grow over with grass, and a new path would be born. In the same way, we want to create a "new path" for our minds. We want to re-direct our thinking. So, when our minds want to go down the worn-out path, we have to purposely choose a new path. Each time we choose that new path, it will become more worn out. In time, it will become a "rut," and what our minds automatically go to.

Practically speaking, how do we re-direct our thinking and where do we direct it to?

- How? We have to make a purposeful choice to say, "I'm not going down that road." We then choose the road we want to go down. That means that when our thoughts begin to go down the old, worn-out path, we have to say, "No." Sometimes, we may have to physically move in order to emotionally re-direct our thinking. In other words, if we're in bed and wake up to a nightmare, we need to get up and go to another room. If we're in a room, maybe we need to walk outside or go to another place. When we re-direct physically, it is easier to re-direct mentally and emotionally.
- Where? Choose ahead of time where you will re-direct. We might go to a special or memorized Scripture. We might go to a special memory rather than a difficult one. We might go to a hymn or worship song, a picture, or a favorite song of ours. Or we might remind ourselves of the "truth" rather than the false thinking.

When my dad was in his last week, he went through some difficult days. My mind is tempted to drift back to those days, and I could focus on those moments and be greatly hurt by them. Or I could remember that special moment when I went to pray for him, and he began praying for me! So, that's what I do. I re-direct my mind from those difficult moments and focus on that special memory. When my mom went through some difficult days in her last weeks and months, it was hard to watch. I could focus on those, or I could re-direct my thinking to those special nights when I played and sang some of her old favorite hymns from Johnny Cash, Tennessee Ernie Ford, and George Beverly Shea. Now I have a voice that only a mom could love, but that is a special memory. You can do the same thing.

Now that we know we have to re-direct our thinking, here are some of the "false" thoughts that need to be replaced with "truth:"

- **"People closest to us can escape death."** Maybe we don't say it out loud, but we think it. We know from the news and life around us that people are dying, but somehow, we think it will never happen to our loved ones, our family. We think our family will escape tragedy and loss. But the truth is that we all face death at some point; no one escapes it.
- **"Good people (Christians) don't face tragedy or death."** Sometimes we get this idea from a pastor, a church, or a Bible study leader. But often it just seems "right" to us in our minds. We've been taught that if you honor God, He honors you and takes care of you. So, in our minds, that means "bad things" shouldn't happen to "good people." Because it's so hard to see this happen, tons of books have been written about it. In one way or another, they ask, "Why do bad things happen to good people?" But the truth is, bad things do happen to good people. The Bible is full of stories like that.
- **"Young people aren't supposed to die,"** or **"My child isn't supposed to die before I do."** We talked about this earlier when we talked about the death of a child. It just seems like children are innocent and haven't lived enough life yet. In our minds, they shouldn't have to face tragedy and death. But death does come to all ages. It is part of this "fallen" world.
- **"If I knew 'why,' I'd be better."** I hear this often and see people searching desperately for answers. You know what I've learned through the years? It doesn't help. For every "why" question answered, another one pops up. The search becomes never ending. Only when one comes to a point that they don't have to have all the answers or know all the "whys," can they move forward.
- **"It's my fault! If only I had..."** We talked about this some earlier when we talked about guilt and the "if only." Most of our guilt is "false guilt." We somehow wish or think that we could have changed the

outcome... that somehow, we could have stopped the tragedy or the death.

- **"I'm all alone."** I get it; it sure seems that way. But I would lovingly remind you that you're not. If you have God, you are not alone. He is constantly with you. In the 23rd Psalm He says, "Yea, though I walk through the valley of the shadow of death I will fear no evil, for Thou (God) art with me..." Psalm 139 shares the same truth—that God is with us, no matter where we are.

  With that being said, I know that sometimes we need someone we can see and touch. I think of a little girl who was having a nightmare and her mom came in to comfort her. The mom knelt by the bed, talked with her, prayed with her, and gently held her. After time, the mom got up to leave and the daughter cried out, "Don't leave me!" The mom reminded her that God was with her and would watch over her. The girl replied back, "I know, but I need a God with skin on." I chuckled when I heard that story. But she's right. Sometimes we do need a "God with skin on." So, I pray that God will bring some trusted friends into your life. Maybe they will come from your church, your family, or your community.

  Here are a few practical tips to help with loneliness that I've learned through the years and that people have shared with me:

  - Find something special to do: a craft, a hobby, reading, exercise, etc.
  - Spend some time in the Bible and listening to the old hymns and praise music.
  - Find a place to volunteer and help others—church or community.
  - Join a group or mission.

- **"There's no hope."** I know it seems dark. I know it seems empty. But there is hope. The light will come out again. Lovingly I tell you, that as long as you have God, you have hope. I've seen people find hope; I've seen them find purpose and joy again. I've watched God heal broken heart after broken heart.

What else keeps the pain alive?

Friends and family who hurt us

Sometimes friends and family say the wrong things or hurtful things, because they just don't know better. Sometimes they grieve in such different ways that it appears that they don't care, and that keeps the pain alive.

At other times, friends and family purposely lash out with hurtful words and actions. Too often, there is fighting over money and possessions. I've been in homes where people are fighting over "things" before the person has even passed. I've been in homes, funeral homes, and cemeteries where I've had to break up fights and even call the police. These things bring tremendous pain and only add to the grief that is already there. In hurts like these, forgiveness and boundaries become an important part of our journey toward healing.

Unforgiveness

Speaking of unforgiveness, it is one of the things that keeps pain alive. Without forgiveness, there is no healing. When we fail to forgive, it's like a poison or cancer that eats us alive. We cannot heal or move forward with unforgiveness as a part of our lives.

Sometimes we are hesitant to forgive because we're afraid "they will get off the hook" or that we're saying what they did was okay. But that's not true at all. We must trust that God will still hold them accountable and that God will deal with them in His time and way (Romans 12:17-19, Hebrews 10:30).

I am simply saying that if God forgave me, I can forgive others. Ephesians 4 says it this way,

"31 Let all bitterness, wrath, anger, clamor, and evil speaking be put away from you, with all malice. 32 And be *kind to one another, tenderhearted, forgiving one another, even as God in Christ forgave you*." The truth is that I've been forgiven far more than I deserve. When I remember that, I find it easier to forgive others.

Even the Lord's Prayer or "Our Father," that we recite and know so well, says this,

9 In this manner, therefore, pray:
Our Father in heaven,
Hallowed be Your name.
10 Your kingdom come.
Your will be done
On earth as *it is* in heaven.
11 Give us this day our daily bread.
12 And forgive us our debts,
As we forgive our debtors.
13 And do not lead us into temptation,
But deliver us from the evil one.
For Yours is the kingdom and the power and the glory forever. Amen.

14 "*For if you forgive men their trespasses, your heavenly Father will also forgive you. 15 But if you do not forgive men their trespasses, neither will your Father forgive your trespasses*.

Remember, when we fail to forgive, we don't punish them; we punish ourselves. Unforgiveness will steal our joy and peace. Unforgiveness will keep the pain alive.

Let me add these two last things as a balance. One, the idea of "forgive and forget" is not a biblical one and is not the test of whether we have forgiven or not. We can't simply "forget" deep or ongoing hurt; the pain and hurt can remain in our minds. But forgiveness means that we no longer hold it against them, and it no longer enslaves us. Second, even after forgiveness there is a place for boundaries, including distancing ourselves from the offender. A trusted friend, pastor, or counselor can help us more with this.

Living by emotions

It's okay to be emotional; loss brings a tangled ball of emotions! But when we live by our emotions, it keeps us from moving forward. Emotions go up and down like a roller coaster. So, if we live by our emotions, our lives will go up and down like a roller coaster.

Emotions can be a part of our lives; they just can't lead us. I like to use the illustration of a train. The train can have an engine, cars, and a caboose.

The engine pulls the train, the cars follow, and the caboose brings up the rear. That's what we know and expect. But what if we were to move the caboose to the front and ask it to pull the train. Would that work? No! There's no way the caboose could pull the train. It would be a disaster and end in a wreck.

Our emotions are like the caboose. They can bring up the rear, or be along for the ride, but they cannot lead. If our emotions lead our lives, it will end in a certain wreck.

The truth is there will be times that we have to make some hard choices or take some difficult steps. We won't feel like it, but we must do it to move forward. We may have to choose to forgive or reach out. We may simply have to choose to get out of the house or join someone for lunch.

Again, it's okay for emotions to be a part of our lives; we just can't live by them.

Trying to control everyone & everything

Some of us are "control freaks." We want to control everything. Death and loss are especially hard for us. They are a reminder that we really don't control everything, and that we can't stop death or loss from happening.

I remember when I was a fire chaplain and talked with law enforcement after one of their own was gunned down. It was a domestic violence call, with some added risks. Two officers arrived and staged just like they were trained. While waiting for backup, the officers were shot by the husband who had perched on the rooftop with a scoped rifle. You can imagine the hurt, pain, and anger of their fellow officers. I still remember one of those officers sitting in my office. He kept saying, "They did everything they were supposed to do. They did just what they were trained to do. How did this happen?" You see, law enforcement is taught to take immediate control of the scene and dictate the outcome. But this day it didn't work. On this day, the tragedy couldn't be stopped.

Death and loss have a way of doing that. They remind us that we're not in control. We can't always stop or change things. Until we realize this and surrender, the pain will continue. A book in the Bible, Ecclesiastes, reminds us that there is a time and season for everything, including death. It will come to all of us one day.

Refusing to let go

Some want to hold on as if their loved one is still living or is coming back; they don't want to accept the reality of the death. They try to keep things exactly the same as they were, and refuse to move forward. We're not talking about holding on to memories or cherished moments; those are important. We're talking about holding on to the hope that their lost loved one will return or that things will remain the way they were.

To heal, we have to come to a point where we realize that they are not coming back. They will not pull up in the drive, sit down with us at the table tonight, or crawl into bed beside us. This is a hard truth, but it is an important step in healing.

Disbelief and refusal to accept the loss are very common early on and can continue to pop up throughout the grief journey. But if that refusal dominates our journey as we continue, it will keep the pain alive. It will keep us from adjusting to our new world without our loved one; it will keep us from beginning a new life; it will keep us anchored to the death.

As we heal and grow, we will learn to hold on to the memories and connections while we begin a new journey at the same time.

Isolating yourself

It's tempting; very tempting. But this is one of the most dangerous things we can do. It invites darkness, depression, and hopelessness. We need God, and we need others to walk with us. God didn't make us to walk through this journey alone. That's why I love the 23rd Psalm where he says, "Yea, though I walk through the valley of the shadow of death, I will fear no evil; For You *are* with me; Your rod and Your staff, they comfort me."

I remember a gentleman who lost two of his loved ones in a tragic accident. I could see the growing temptation to withdraw and isolate himself. We talked about isolation in the grief class, and one on one. I warned him again and again about the dangers. But he insisted on separating himself from others. Just as warned, he began to spiral out of control. His pain grew like crazy.

Don't be like him. Allow others to be a part of your life. Work hard to get out of the house, to join others. Let God walk with you. Run <u>to</u> Him, not away from Him.

Legal paperwork, estate, etc.

When I first started my hospice chaplain work, I didn't realize all that comes after the death! There is so much paperwork, loose ends to tie up, and the never-ending estate issues. Much of it can linger on for months, or even years. It adds such a burden to the pain of grief.

I remember when my dad passed away, the bank was kind enough to inform the Social Security Administration that my dad had passed and returned his check. The only problem was that they also returned my mom's check, stating that she too had died. It took months and months of time to convince the Social Security Administration that she was still alive and to get her checks started again. This just added hurt to the pain that was already there.

For many, the sale of the house or farm just adds to the loss. Not only have you lost the one you love, but now you lose the gathering place, the place where so many memories were made. May God help you in this part of your journey.

HOW DO I MOVE FORWARD?

That's the big question, isn't it? How do I hold on to the memories and connection of the ones I love, but move forward? Not "move on," but move forward. Throughout the book, I've mixed in some "moving forward" truths, but here I want to share some very specific, direct truths to help you:

Don't get "anchored" to the death

Some people can't get past that day, or that moment. They stay anchored to it. But if we stay anchored to something we can't move forward.

How do you know if you're anchored to the moment of death or loss? If you find yourself constantly rehearsing it or re-living every detail, then you're anchored to it. If you think back on your loved one's life and you focus on their last week or month more than all the other memories, then you're anchored to the moment.

Do me a favor? Get a piece of paper or use a blank page at the end of this book. Put a little black dot on it. Now look away for a moment—out the window, to the other side of the room, or at another person. After a few minutes, look back at the paper or page. What do you see? A black dot!

That's human nature—to see the black dot. It stands out. But... look at all the white around it! The dot is small compared to it. But somehow, we see the black dot, not the white paper. Our eyes become "anchored" to the black dot.

Part of moving forward is seeing the "white paper," getting our eyes off of the black dot. The "white paper" represents the blessings, the cherished memories, the special moments, and life in the midst of death and loss.

When we get "anchored" to the moment of death, all we can see is the black dot. Everything else disappears. I remember a young man whose father died. He was overwhelmed by grief and all he could see was the black dot. He couldn't see his wife, his young children, his friends, or other blessings around him. His focus on the "black dot" became so severe that he even thought about taking his own life. But look at all he, and his family, would have lost!

How do you see the "white paper?" People often find it helpful to keep a "Book of Blessings" or a journal. One man I was helping sat down with his wife and found over 50 blessings in the midst of heartache and tragedy.

Often, following a death or loss, I will see a new child born. It's almost as if God knows we need to be reminded that there is life, there is new birth, and that there can be joy. The blessings are there; we just miss them.

Don't get anchored to the "black dot;" look for the "white paper."

Focus on the "windshield" not the "rearview mirror"

What would happen if you drove looking in the rearview mirror the whole time? Exactly!

Now, the rearview mirror isn't bad. In fact, it's very important. We need it, and we need to check it pretty often. But we can't drive looking at it the whole time. The result would be disastrous.

In a similar way, we can't live life continually looking at the past. The result would be disastrous. I've seen people try it, and it doesn't work. Things are not the same now; and unfortunately, they never will be. I wish it wasn't true, but it is.

It doesn't mean that we can't remember the past or celebrate the past. It means we can't live there. Just like it's okay to check the rearview mirror (in fact, necessary), it's okay to "check" the past—in fact, necessary. We just can't dwell there.

So, we must look ahead through the windshield, to see what God still has in store for us. There is still life to live—people who need us, and a purpose God still has for us. I bet even your loved one would want you to keep living life and moving forward.

Remember, it's okay to check the rearview mirror... just don't live there.

Be thankful for what you've had, rather than focus on what you don't have

It's easy, especially in the loss of a child, to focus on what "could have been" or what you will be missing. But that will only lead to more heartache and frustration. It will also rob you of the joy found in memories and precious moments that you have already experienced.

I know you didn't have them long enough (it's never long enough). But, in those days, months, or years, God has blessed you with a lot of memories and precious moments. Don't let those get pushed out because you are grieving "what will never be." Remember the laughter; remember the adventures; remember their impact on you. Cherish those moments.

Remember the black dot and the white paper? Here the white paper is all the blessings that you have enjoyed through the days, months, and years.

One couple had their child for only four days. I can't imagine the hurt and disappointment. But they chose to cherish every minute of holding him, talking to him, and singing to him. When he passed, they thanked God for those four days. They thanked God for letting them feel their boy in their arms, for getting to hold him close, and to soak in his presence. They focused on what they had, rather than on what "could have been."

Don't let the "loss" keep you from the "blessings."

Do the "next thing;" one step at a time

We've said this many times throughout the book, but it's worth saying again— "one step at a time." I used to say, "One day at a time." But I've learned that sometimes that is too much! Sometimes it's just one hour or one minute at a time.

Grief and loss can be overwhelming. The only way to make it is one step at a time. It might be the first step of getting up in the morning, eating breakfast, and spending some time with God. Once you have completed that first step, then you can look at the next step.

During my wife's battle with cancer, our mantra became *"Don't Run Ahead of God."* It was a simple reminder to take it one step at a time, trusting Him. We found that God would give us the grace and strength when we needed it, not before. When we ran ahead of God, we would outrun His grace. We would become worried, fearful, or overwhelmed.

Soon after a death, there is a lot to be done. One need after another piles up. It can be overwhelming. How do you tackle so much? One step at a time. It's like the old saying, "How do you eat an elephant? One bite at a time."

Celebrate their life

Part of remembering your loved one and cherishing those special moments is finding a way to celebrate their life. Here are some ways that others have celebrated their loved ones:

- Keep a special item, piece of jewelry, etc.
- Plant a tree or flower; place a bench/special object
- Create a picture book or a picture wall
- Make a special piece of jewelry to remember
- Make a memory quilt, bear, pillow, etc.
- Have a special place of memory
- Start a movement, ministry, or scholarship fund in their memory
- Live out their legacy and values
- Light a candle or leave an empty chair at a family gathering/holiday; visit a special place that they/you enjoyed
- Plan a family or friend gathering with time to share memories

Share with others

It's important for us to talk about the pain and grief that we're going through. We need someone to share with; it's part of the grieving process. It might be a grief support group; it might be a close friend(s); it might be family. But we all need someone. Holding the loss and pain in is dangerous. If we hold it in, the dam will break sooner or later and all the hurt and grief that has piled up will come flooding out (remember the story of the lady at the beginning of the book).

We can help our family and friends by bringing up our loved ones first, giving them permission to talk about them. Sometimes our family and friends are afraid to talk about our loved ones because they are afraid that it will make us cry or hurt us. But I've learned through the years that it hurts more not to talk about them, than it does to talk about them. Talking about our loved ones keeps the memories alive and lets us express our love for the ones we lost. As we share, God brings healing.

As you share with others, know that it's ok to be choosy about who and how many you share with. Some people are just nosy or "gossips." There are some who are more interested in themselves than you. Avoid those people. But there are trusted people around you; share with them. If by chance you don't have one of those people, ask God to bring one into your life. I have seen Him do that again and again. By the way, God might want to use you to be that trusted friend for another.

Another way that you can share is by writing. Write out your prayer, write in a journal, or write a letter to your loved one. Prayer is simply talking with God and listening to Him. When it's hard to say a prayer, some people find it easier to write a prayer. It's kind of like you and God writing letters back and forth. Journaling gives you a place to pour out your heart—to share your struggles and joys, your heartaches and blessings. Writing a letter to your loved one allows you to say "goodbye," to say the things you wish you could have said, or to share your ongoing life with them. All of these help us to share. I've learned through the years that some people can do this easier in writing than they can in speaking.

Listen to or play music

Music has a way of speaking to our soul. I love music, and God has used it many times to speak to me. It has provided comfort, strength, and peace. I have some special songs and favorite groups that I listen to over and over again. I bet you do too. Download them to your phone, download a music app, or keep a CD handy.

Build some time into your day to listen to music—maybe as you start your day, or as you lie down at night for sleep. Listen to music throughout the day, especially if it's a difficult day or a difficult moment.

Reading

Reading also has a way of speaking to us. It might be an escape, or a much-needed word of comfort and encouragement.

I personally love to read through the Psalms in the Bible (right in the middle of your Bible). They are filled with all of the emotions of life. Sometimes David and the other psalmists are "higher than a kite" because everything is going right, and sometimes they are "lower than a snake's belly" because everything is going wrong. They are honest about life. I like that, and I see myself in the Psalms. God has used them again and again to bring comfort, peace, strength, and encouragement.

Some like to read through a devotional book that shares a Scripture and a few thoughts or stories to help explain the meaning. You can find many that have a daily reading to make it easy for you.

You may just enjoy reading in general. Some find that it's a good "escape," a way to think about something besides their loss and daily challenges. You might want to create a reading nook or set aside a special place.

Begin to give to others

It seems odd to help others when you feel like you have nothing to give. Your first thought might be, "I can't do that!" But you would be surprised; I have seen this step help people move forward and bring healing more than almost any other.

Years ago, a mom lost her son to suicide. You can imagine the deep pain. She and I talked many times in the following days. About a month after the tragedy, another young man in the community took his life. That second mom came to me crying out for help. At a risk, I reached out to the first mom and asked if she might help this second mom. After some hesitation, she agreed. What took place in the weeks and months ahead was amazing. The first mom was a tremendous help to the second mom. She knew firsthand the hurt and pain; she knew the difficult journey. But it did something more. It began to bring healing to the first mom. The more she gave, the more she healed.

I have since seen this repeated many times over. Why does it help? Because helping others helps us process our own loss and pain; it also takes our eyes off ourselves.

Begin praying and looking for a place to volunteer or minister. It might be at your church, a local ministry or community group, or your neighborhood. Begin small, but begin. As you give, you will begin to heal.

Spend time with God

I don't know where you're at in your faith, but I know that I couldn't make it a single day without Him.

Have there been times when I wondered if He heard me? Sure! Have there been times when I wondered if He was at work? Sure! But in time, I learned that He did hear me and that He was at work.

I learned from Martha in John 11 to run <u>to</u> God, not away from Him. I found that the greater the hurt, the greater my need for Him. So, I began to set aside regular time each day to talk with Him in prayer and hear from Him in Bible reading. I began to talk with Him throughout the day. I began to pray like I breathed—constantly!

You may say, "I don't know how to pray." Just talk to Him in honest, simple words. And when you are not sure what to say or don't have the words, He knows... He hears your heart.

You may say, "I don't know how to read the Bible or where to start." Maybe begin by reading the Psalms (in the middle of your Bible or on your Bible app). You could just read one psalm a day or as much as you feel like. A simple guide is to read the psalm that matches whatever day it is—in other words, if it's the 12th, read Psalm 12. On the 13th, read Psalm 13.

Spending time with God will be one of the most important things you can do to move forward.

DAY TO DAY PRACTICAL HELP

As we wrap up the book, let me share some "practical tips" that I've learned from others and in my own journey. They are simple, day-to-day helps.

Plan an "escape" if attending an event

You need to get out of the house, and you want to take that next step, but you're afraid of how long you will last at an event or if you can even stay at all. So, it's important that you plan an escape.

The first plan is to take your own car. Why is that? So that you're not trapped. If you ride with someone else, you can't leave until they do. You're trapped. But if you take your own car, you can leave the event when you're ready... whether it's thirty minutes into it or five seconds into it.

If you go as a couple or with a friend, make sure you clearly communicate that you may need to leave on a moment's notice, and that your friend clearly understands how urgent the need is. It's even a good idea to come up with a signal or "code word." If I'm with my wife and I pat her back (or her leg if we're sitting down), she knows that means that we need to go...now!

Sitting near the back and at the end of a row is also a good idea. You probably don't want to sit up in the front or in the middle of a row! If you urgently need to get out, you're trapped. If you had to leave, those places would be very difficult to get out of and leaving would make a scene.

Arrive late, leave early; begin small

I've learned that going back to church can be overwhelming and difficult for many. Sometimes you are mobbed by well-meaning, loving people. They keep coming up to you and asking how you are doing. They may even want to "hug on you." If you're not ready for all of that, here's a suggestion: arrive late and leave early (don't tell your pastor I said that; but it does help). You can also slip into the back and slip out early—not forever, but just to get used to it again. Your church may even have a cry room or balcony that you could quietly slip into.

I also encourage people to begin small. Maybe start with a small Bible study, Sunday night, or Wednesday night rather than a large Sunday morning service. Small steps first, then bigger steps as you adjust.

This principle can apply to other events as well, not just church. Arrive late; leave early; start small.

Scale back on family events or gatherings

It's good to have family events and gatherings. We need family and others in our lives! But be willing to scale back. The holidays don't have to be huge meals with tons of people. Family gatherings don't have to be all of the extended family; they can be limited to just the immediate family this time. The meal doesn't have to be some elaborate, all day cooking event. It could be a simple meal, or even prepared food brought in.

I know one family who traditionally had a large family gathering every fall that would be 50-60 people. After their loved one died, they still wanted to have the gathering but didn't have the energy or strength to do something that big. So, they simplified the event and scaled back to only 15-20 close family members. It was still a special time, but not so overwhelming.

This same principle can be applied to other things as well, like sending Christmas cards. It's not a failure to scale back. It's a recognition that there has been a major life change and I need to adjust.

Set boundaries with family and friends

Sometimes family and friends can be "too helpful," or too pushy. They want to tell you what to do or how to do it. They may visit too often or even "camp out" at your home to keep you from being alone. They mean well, but they bring added stress. That's where we need to put boundaries in place and hold to our own desires and convictions.

Other times, family or friends bring hurts and ongoing "drama" (like we talked about before). That's not what you need when you're already dealing with all the emotions and effects of your loss. During times like this, don't be afraid to put some boundaries in place. It might mean limiting their time with you or their access to your family. It might mean limiting communication, either directly or in social media.

People may try to make you feel guilty about putting boundaries in place, but don't let them. The Bible has numerous examples of "boundaries" being put in place. So, don't let people tell you that if you put boundaries in place that means that you haven't forgiven them. You can forgive someone and still wisely put boundaries in place.

Hopefully the boundaries will be temporary and God can reconcile the relationship(s) or people will ease up. But it may take a while, and honestly it may never happen this side of heaven. Keep the boundaries in place as long as you need.

Balance time alone and time with others

Some of us naturally like to spend time with others, and some of us like to be alone. Some of us are "recharged" by being with other people, and some of us are "recharged" by having "alone" time. God made us that way, and that's okay.

But I've learned through the years that there needs to be a healthy balance. For those who love to be with people, they may rarely spend time alone. They are busy going from one event to the next and constantly surrounding themselves with people. Without realizing it, they often don't take time to grieve or process their loss.

For those who like to be alone, they run the risk of isolation like we've talked about before. In that isolation, they dwell on the loss and are drawn into the darkness.

It's okay to be yourself, but find a healthy balance. Include others in your life if you're a "loner," or find some "alone" time if you're a constant "people" person.

Be cautious of "big decisions" and major changes in the first year

You've probably heard this before, but it's a very important warning. Because we are often "blurry" in our thinking and overwhelmed by emotions, we can easily make decisions or make a move that we later regret and costs us dearly. It might be a financial, home, lifestyle, or a relationship decision that we need to be careful of.

During this time of loss, I've known some who have been taken advantage of by scams and dishonesty; I know of others who have moved or made major changes, and then later regretted it. I don't want to see that happen to you.

It's best to put major decisions off. But you may have no choice. If you must, ask the counsel of a trusted friend. Ask someone who is outside of the emotional loss and can see things objectively and clearly. It might be a trusted friend, pastor, counselor, or accountant. Ask God to help direct you to the right person. Many times, they are already in our lives.

Be very careful of entering into another relationship too soon

This expands on the previous caution. I see this happen often. You can be lonely, hurting, and eager for companionship. You may need someone to notice or hear you. Because of where you're at, your guard is down and you don't see things like you normally would. It can open you up to an unhealthy relationship that "covers" the grief but brings added hurt, or even abuse. It can even cause one to begin a physical relationship, trying to capture the intimacy that has been lost. Please beware.

Write out a prayer, journal, or write a letter to your loved one

I've mentioned it before, but I wanted to mention it again. Writing can be very helpful in your healing. You don't have to be a great writer to do this, just willing. There's something about putting your thoughts down on paper that helps you see the blessings, process the thoughts, and express your heart. Give it a try!

FINAL WORDS

Thank you for letting me share my heart and life with you. I hope and pray that this book has provided some guidance and healing to your journey. Know that you are much loved and prayed for.

On the following pages I've provided some Scriptures that have helped me and numerous others. I pray that they will help you.

If you would like to take a small group through this book, I have provided a "Small Group Leader's Guide" after the Scriptures.

"He heals the brokenhearted
And binds up their wounds." -Psalm 147:3

"Weeping may endure for a night, But joy comes in the morning." -Psalm 30:5b

SCRIPTURES OF COMFORT

PSALM 23

The LORD is my shepherd;
I shall not want.
2 He makes me to lie down in green pastures;
He leads me beside the still waters.
3 He restores my soul;
He leads me in the paths of righteousness
For His name's sake.
4 Yea, though I walk through the valley of the shadow of death,
I will fear no evil;
For You are with me;
Your rod and Your staff, they comfort me.
5 You prepare a table before me in the presence of my enemies;
You anoint my head with oil;
My cup runs over.
6 Surely goodness and mercy shall follow me
All the days of my life;
And I will dwell in the house of the LORD forever.

2 Corinthians 1:3-4

3 Blessed be the God and Father of our Lord Jesus Christ, the Father of
mercies and God of all comfort, 4 who comforts us in all our tribulation,
that we may be able to comfort those who are in any trouble, with the
comfort with which we ourselves are comforted by God.

Psalm 46:1-2a

1 God is our refuge and strength,
A very present help in trouble.
2 Therefore we will not fear...

Matthew 11:28

28 Come to Me, all you who labor and are heavy laden, and I will give you rest.

John 14:27

27 Peace I leave with you, My peace I give to you; not as the world gives do I give to you. Let not your heart be troubled, neither let it be afraid.

Psalm 147:3

3 He heals the brokenhearted
And binds up their wounds.

Psalm 30:5b

5 Weeping may endure for a night, But joy [comes] in the morning.

Psalm 34:18

18 The LORD is near to those who have a broken heart...

Matthew 5:4

4 Blessed are those who mourn, For they shall be comforted.

1 Peter 5:7

7 casting all your care upon Him, for He cares for you.

Philippians 4:6-7

6 Be anxious for nothing, but in everything by prayer and supplication, with thanksgiving, let your requests be made known to God; 7 and the peace of God, which surpasses all understanding, will guard your hearts and minds through Christ Jesus.

John 11:17-36

Now Martha, as soon as she heard that Jesus was coming, went and met Him, but Mary was sitting in the house. 21 Now Martha said to Jesus,

“Lord, if You had been here, my brother would not have died. 22 But even
now I know that whatever You ask of God, God will give You.”
23 Jesus said to her, “Your brother will rise again.”
24 Martha said to Him, “I know that he will rise again in the resurrection at
the last day.”
25 Jesus said to her, “I am the resurrection and the life. He who believes
in Me, though he may die, he shall live. 26 And whoever lives and believes
in Me shall never die. Do you believe this?”
27 She said to Him, “Yes, Lord, I believe that You are the Christ, the Son of
God, who is to come into the world.”
28 And when she had said these things, she went her way and secretly
called Mary her sister, saying, “The Teacher has come and is calling for
you.” 29 As soon as she heard that, she arose quickly and came to
Him. 30 Now Jesus had not yet come into the town, but was in the place
where Martha met Him. 31 Then the Jews who were with her in the house,
and comforting her, when they saw that Mary rose up quickly and went
out, followed her, saying, “She is going to the tomb to weep there.”
32 Then, when Mary came where Jesus was, and saw Him, she fell down
at His feet, saying to Him, “Lord, if You had been here, my brother would
not have died.”
33 Therefore, when Jesus saw her weeping, and the Jews who came with
her weeping, He groaned in the spirit and was troubled. 34 And He
said, “Where have you laid him?”
They said to Him, “Lord, come and see.” 35 Jesus wept. 36 Then the Jews
said, “See how He loved him!”

Ecclesiastes 3:1-4

1 To everything there is a season,
A time for every purpose under heaven:
2 A time to be born,
And a time to die;
A time to plant,
And a time to pluck what is planted;

3 A time to kill,
And a time to heal;
A time to break down,
And a time to build up;
4 A time to weep,
And a time to laugh;
A time to mourn,
And a time to dance;

SCRIPTURES ON HEAVEN

John 14:1-6

1 “Let not your heart be troubled; you believe in God, believe also in
Me. 2 In My Father’s house are many mansions; if it were not so, I would
have told you. I go to prepare a place for you. 3 And if I go and prepare a
place for you, I will come again and receive you to Myself; that where I
am, there you may be also. 4 And where I go you know, and the way you
know.”
5 Thomas said to Him, “Lord, we do not know where You are going, and
how can we know the way?”
6 Jesus said to him, “I am the way, the truth, and the life. No one comes to
the Father except through Me.

Revelation 21:3-5

3 And I heard a loud voice from heaven saying, “Behold, the tabernacle of
God is with men, and He will dwell with them, and they shall be His
people. God Himself will be with them and be their God. 4 And God will
wipe away every tear from their eyes; there shall be no more death, nor
sorrow, nor crying. There shall be no more pain, for the former things have
passed away.”
5 Then He who sat on the throne said, “Behold, I make all things new.” And
He said to me, “Write, for these words are true and faithful.”

Luk 23:42-43

42 Then he said to Jesus, "Lord, remember me when You come into Your
kingdom." 43 And Jesus said to him, "Assuredly, I say to you, today you will
be with Me in Paradise."

2 Corinthians 5:4, 8

4 For we who are in this tent [earthly body] groan, being burdened, not
because we want to be unclothed, but further clothed, that mortality

[death] may be swallowed up by life. ... 8 We are confident, yes, well pleased rather to be absent from the body and to be present with the Lord.

SCRIPTURES ON ANGER AND FORGIVENESS

Matthew 18
21 Then Peter came to Him and said, “Lord, how often shall my brother
sin against me, and I forgive him? Up to seven times?”
22 Jesus said to him, “I do not say to you, up to seven times, but up to
seventy times seven. 23 Therefore the kingdom of heaven is like a certain
king who wanted to settle accounts with his servants. 24 And when he
had begun to settle accounts, one was brought to him who owed him ten
thousand talents. 25 But as he was not able to pay, his master
commanded that he be sold, with his wife and children and all that he
had, and that payment be made. 26 The servant therefore fell down before
him, saying, ‘Master, have patience with me, and I will pay you all.’ 27 Then
the master of that servant was moved with compassion, released him,
and forgave him the debt.
28 “But that servant went out and found one of his fellow servants who
owed him a hundred denarii; and he laid hands on him and took him by
the throat, saying, ‘Pay me what you owe!’ 29 So his fellow servant fell
down at his feet and begged him, saying, ‘Have patience with me, and I
will pay you all.’ 30 And he would not, but went and threw him into prison
till he should pay the debt. 31 So when his fellow servants saw what had
been done, they were very grieved, and came and told their master all that
had been done. 32 Then his master, after he had called him, said to him,
‘You wicked servant! I forgave you all that debt because you begged
me. 33 Should you not also have had compassion on your fellow servant,
just as I had pity on you?’ 34 And his master was angry, and delivered him
to the torturers until he should pay all that was due to him.
35 “So My heavenly Father also will do to you if each of you, from his heart,
does not forgive his brother his trespasses.”

Matthew 6
9 Our Father in heaven,
Hallowed be Your name.
10 Your kingdom come.
Your will be done
On earth as it is in heaven.
11 Give us this day our daily bread.
12 And forgive us our debts,
As we forgive our debtors.
13 And do not lead us into temptation,
But deliver us from the evil one.
For Yours is the kingdom and the power and the glory forever. Amen.

14 "For if you forgive men their trespasses, your heavenly Father will also
forgive you. 15 But if you do not forgive men their trespasses, neither will
your Father forgive your trespasses.

Ephesians 4
26 "Be angry, and do not sin": do not let the sun go down on your
wrath, 27 nor give place to the devil.

Hebrews 12
14 Pursue peace with all people, and holiness, without which no one will
see the Lord: 15 looking carefully lest anyone fall short of the grace of
God; lest any root of bitterness springing up cause trouble, and by this
many become defiled;

EXAMPLES OF PEOPLE GRIEVING IN THE BIBLE

Jesus in John 11 and Mark 14:32-36 & Luke 22:39-46

Job in the book of Job

David throughout the Psalms

King David in 2 Samuel 12

Naomi in Ruth 1

Hannah in 1 Samuel 1

Hagar in Genesis 21

Jeremiah in Jeremiah 20:7-18 and the book of Lamentations

Elijah in 1 Kings 19:1-12

SMALL GROUP LEADER GUIDE

For years now, I have been leading a 6-week grief support class, sharing these truths that you just read. The response has been tremendous. People have been asking for a book so that these truths could be shared with others individually or in their own 6-week grief support group. This section has been added to help those who want to lead their own group. You will need to purchase a **GriefCare Workbook** for each participant. The workbook is an outline of this book, and is perfect for giving structure and direction to your group time.

A PERSONAL WORD TO YOU, THE LEADER

Thank you for walking with those who are going through such a difficult time in their lives. Few can do what you are doing. Remember, you are here because God called you and equipped you to be here. If you're like me, God has shaped your own heart through pain and loss. God will use that hurt in your own life to help others; He will redeem your pain. Let the One who is the "God of all comfort" and "Prince of Peace" use you.

> ***2 Corinthians 1:3-4***
>
> *3 Blessed be the God and Father of our Lord Jesus Christ, the Father of mercies and God of all comfort, 4 who comforts us in all our tribulation, that we may be able to comfort those who are in any trouble, with the comfort with which we ourselves are comforted by God.*

You will be a facilitator or discussion leader, not a "fixer." The pressure is NOT on you to "fix" or "heal" their broken hearts; that is God's job (and He is quite good at it! I've seen Him do it many times). Your job is to be compassionately present, to prayerfully usher them into God's presence, and to lead them to find the hope and healing of Christ.

As a facilitator, I would encourage you to ask open-ended, leading questions to invite them into the discussion. As the group becomes more comfortable with one another and you, they will share more and more. Your responses and spirit will greatly encourage or discourage interaction.

As I mentioned earlier, the book you just read will give you structure and guidance for the **GRIEFCARE WORKBOOK** (sold separately). In addition, some key Scriptures were provided for you just before this section. I greatly encourage you to weave these biblical truths into every session. Your sensitivity to the Holy Spirit and knowing His Word will be a great help.

In addition to this guide, I would highly recommend the book Effective Grief Counseling: A Guide to Counseling and Supporting the Grieving by Dr. Tony Lewis (Amazon). There are additional recommended books listed at the end of this section (for leaders and others). I hope that they will be of good help to you.

THE PURPOSE

The workbook (and this book) was written with a desire to help the grieving know what to expect and how to move forward. I have a deep conviction that a grief group should not simply rehash the pain week after week. This does more harm than good. A grief group should be a safe place to share, a place to find compassion, and a place to grieve. But it should also be a place to find direction and healing, a place to learn how to move forward.

ABOUT THE GRIEFCARE WORKBOOK

Every person will need their own GriefCare Workbook. The workbook will provide an outline that will walk them through their six-week journey. There is plenty of room for notes; I encourage them to jot notes so that they can come back to these truths in the weeks and months ahead (when people are grieving they don't always remember or process all that they hear).

I have purposely written the workbook in an outline form so that you, the leader, can interact with those in the class (rather than lecture at them). I want to give you the "bones," and then let you "flesh" it out using truths from God's Word, this book, and your own experience. This allows you to personalize the workbook while still covering important truths.

You will also notice that there are no "session" breaks. This is on purpose. I've learned that each group is different and may need to spend more time on one truth or section than another. This gives you that flexibility. Not having a specific page that you must get to each meeting allows you to take your time and meet needs. Now, obviously, you will want to finish the curriculum by the end of six weeks, but you have the flexibility to adjust time where needed. If you'd like a general guideline, you can use this:

- Session 1: into the early part of the EMOTIONS & EFFECTS OF GRIEF
- Session 2: review of Session 1 and continuing the EMOTIONS & EFFECTS OF GRIEF
- Session 3: finishing the EMOTIONS & EFFECTS and beginning CHALLENGES OF A DEATH OF...
- Session 4: finishing CHALLENGES and beginning WHAT KEEPS THE PAIN ALIVE
- Session 5: continuing WHAT KEEPS THE PAIN ALIVE and entering MOVING FORWARD
- Session 6: finishing what is left. I began providing a "fellowship meal" at this last session as well, and it has become a special moment for the class.

TEACHING AND MINISTRY MOMENTS

The outline is filled with numerous opportunities to minister and teach biblical/grief truths. God's Spirit, God's Word, and this book will help you.

While walking through the outline, you will find that there are several key sections that seem to lead to much sharing and discussion.

- "The Emotions and Effects of Grief," especially "Anger," "Guilt" and "Loneliness" always draw out a lot of sharing and discussion. That's why the "general" guide of sessions allows for a good bit of time on this. I encourage you not to rush through it.
- "The Challenges..." can be the first time a participant begins to share about his/her own specific loss(es). I often ask, "Have any of you been here?" or "How many of you have lost a spouse/child/sibling/etc.?" and raise my hand, prompting them to do so if they have been there.
- "What Keeps the Pain Alive" also seems to be a section that brings out a lot of hurt and discussion.

Finally, let me encourage you to pray in class as led by the Holy Spirit. There are a number of times where the hurt shared is so deep that there is an obvious need for immediate prayer. I always ask, "Can I pray for you right now?" I've never had anyone refuse. When they say, "Yes," I pray on the spot. Often, I will kneel in front of the them or by their side and pray. It is always a powerful moment.

PRACTICAL PREP/HELP FOR THE CLASS

Here are some practical things that you will need to put in place:

- Find a place to meet that is free from distractions and provides a peaceful environment. Make sure that you can see and hear each other well. You might meet at a church or a "neutral" location (like a library or coffee shop after hours). Having easy access to restrooms is a must.
- Provide drinks and snacks if you can (I usually set up a drink/snack table that they can easily access as they enter). Food and drinks are disarming and comforting. Jesus often met around meals.

- Provide a place to: sign in, get a name tag (first name only), and pick up the workbook. I also provide a free book on grief and a list of future classes.
- For the meeting time, I like to sit in a "U" shape at tables so that everyone can see each other well. The tables provide a place to "hide" and hold the workbook/snack/drink/Kleenex (make sure you have several Kleenex boxes spread out). I personally do not like to sit them in a circle; it can leave them feeling too close, trapped, and "naked."
- Advertise ahead: through your church, radio, social media, library, coffee shop, etc.
- Spend much time in prayer before, during, and after. God is the one who will bring those in need and heal their hearts.

BEGINNING THE CLASS & GUIDELINES

At the beginning of class, I introduce myself—briefly sharing about my life, my ministry, and my own experience with grief. This helps them get to know me and makes an initial connection. Next, I share some guidelines for the class:

- No one <u>has</u> to share, but they are welcome to do so. One may attend all 6 sessions and never share a word; or one may share and ask questions from the very beginning. Everyone grieves differently and there is freedom to do that.
- Everything that is shared in this room stays in this room. It is to be a safe place for sharing.
- When someone shares, full attention is directed toward them. No one should interrupt, carry on "side conversations," or distract from their sharing.
- No "preaching" at someone or correcting/judging them. This is a place of grace and healing.

After the guidelines, I begin the night in prayer. Simply pray what is on your heart; a simple, short prayer is often the most effective.

Often, I will begin the class introduction by going around the "U," letting them share their first name and one thing about themselves (it can be anything they choose). There is no pressure for them to share about their loss at this time. In fact, I tell them if we get to you and you cannot share at all, then just point to the person next to you or look at them and we'll skip right over you. After walking through this once, I'll often go around the "U" one more time, asking them to share their first name and what "season of the year" they like most or their "favorite color." This breaks the ice, allows us to hear first names, and eases us into the time together. It is done in a low-pressure, welcoming introduction of one another.

After the introductions, you are ready to begin the time of teaching and discussion. Remember the principles we have talked about. The first session may be more of you leading, with some sharing from the group, because they don't know one another yet and it's all new. But, over time, the group will begin to share more and more as they become more comfortable with you and one another.

Remember, God has put this ministry on your heart. He has called you. You know His comfort firsthand. He will speak through you and love through you. Be very dependent on Him. Without Him, you (and I) are nothing (John 15:5).

SUGGESTED BOOKS:

A Grief Observed by C.S. Lewis

Finding Peace in the Pain by Dr. Tony Lewis

Grieving, Hope and Solace: When a Loved One Dies in Christ by Albert N. Martin

Seasons of Sorrow: The Pain of Loss and Comfort of God by Tim Challies

Safe in the Arms of God by John MacArthur

Missing the Child You Love by H. Norman Wright

SUGGESTED BOOKS FOR LEADERS:

Effective Grief Counseling by Dr. Tony Lewis

Crisis and Trauma Counseling by H. Norman Wright

Recovering from Losses in Life by H. Norman Wright

OTHER BOOKS BY RAY:

I SURVIVED A CHURCH COUP AND SAW THE GOODNESS OF GOD

BIBLIOGRAPHY

"When Someone You Love Dies, There is No Such Thing as Moving On.". Perf. Kelley Lynn. New York City. 31 March 2017. TEDx Talk.

Bakian AV, Chen D, Zhang C, et al. ""A Population-wide Analysis of the Familial Risk of Suicide in Utah"." *Psychological Medicine* (2021): 53(4):1448-1457. doi:10.1017/S0033291721003020.

Hayes, Dr. Terence O. 4 December 2019. FaceBook Post.

Lewis, C.S. *A Grief Observed*. London: Faber and Faber, 1961.

Shakespeare, William. *The Tragedy of Othello, the Moor of Venice. Othelo, Act 3, Scene 3*. 1603. Play.

Worden, J. William. *Grief Counseling and Grief Therapy, Fourth Edition: A Handbook for the Mental Health Practitioner*. New York City: Springer Publishing Company, 2008.

About the Author

Ray A. Johnson

Ray has served over 40 years in full-time ministry as a pastor in Texas, Southern California, and Kentucky. In addition, he served as a fire and hospice chaplain during those years. Ray is the author of another book called I Survived a Church Coup and Saw the Goodness of God.

As the Founder & Director of the Ezekiel Group, Ray has regularly provided trusted, confidential relationships to pastors and hurting people—offering encouragement, counseling, and mentoring.

He is a Certified Christian Grief and Loss Counselor--leading community grief classes, training leaders, and teaching certification classes. Hundreds of people have attended his community grief classes. Ray is well respected in his community for his compassionate care and heart.

Ray and Lauri live in north central Kentucky and have been married for over 39 years. They have 4 grown children and eight grandchildren.

The Ezekiel Group
MINISTRY
"Helping Dry Bones Come to Life"

theezekielgroup.com

www.ingramcontent.com/pod-product-compliance
Lightning Source LLC
LaVergne TN
LVHW090330210926
848480LV00004B/1358

9798996932207